On February 18, 1930—75 years ago—Elm Farm's Ollie was the first cow to fly in an airplane. She was milked while in flight.

Elm Farm Ollie

Can you find these hidden objects?

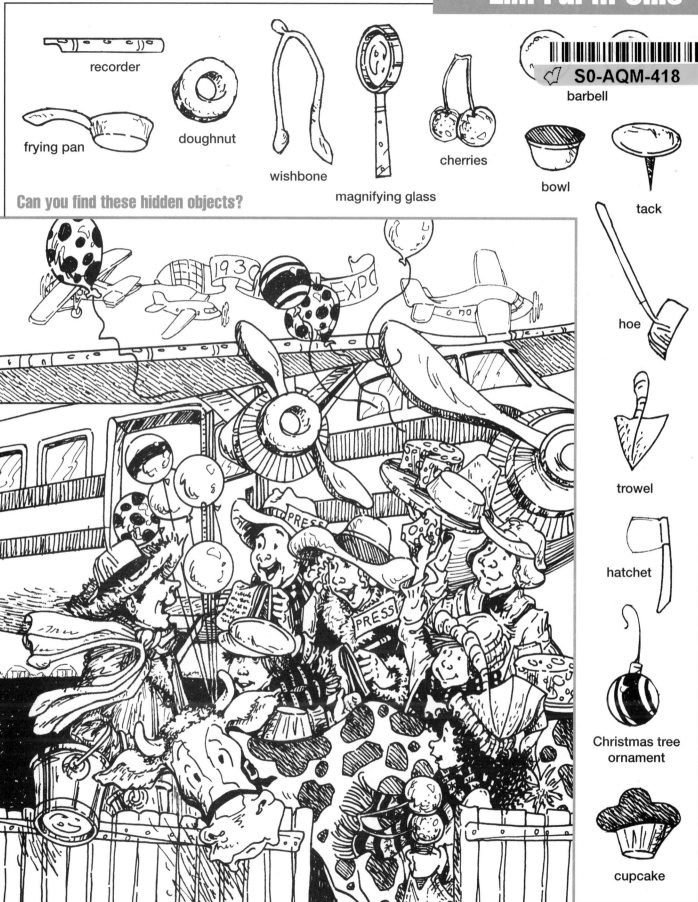

recorder

frying pan

doughnut

wishbone

magnifying glass

cherries

bowl

barbell

tack

hoe

trowel

hatchet

Christmas tree ornament

cupcake

Neighborhood Dog Show

feather

cupcake

ring

snake

wishbone

glove

Can you find these hidden objects?

ice-cream cone

lollipop

doughnut

ladder

banana

spoon

toothbrush

heart

pencil

Deep-Sea Discovery

shovel

toothbrush

pear

pencil

pushpin

slice of pie

candle

Can you find these hidden objects?

slice of cake

artist's brush

spatula

spoon

mushroom

tack

National Pet Week is May 1–7.

goblet

magnet

needle

mallet

scrub brush

pennant

diamond

Can you find these hidden objects?

leaf

funnel

ice-cream bar

crescent moon

paintbrush

nail

Highlights®

tweezers

bird

comb

glove

banana

Can you find these hidden objects?

feather

paper clip

toothbrush

needle

fish

spoon

teacup

Highlights®

The Iditarod Trail Sled Dog Race begins on March 5.

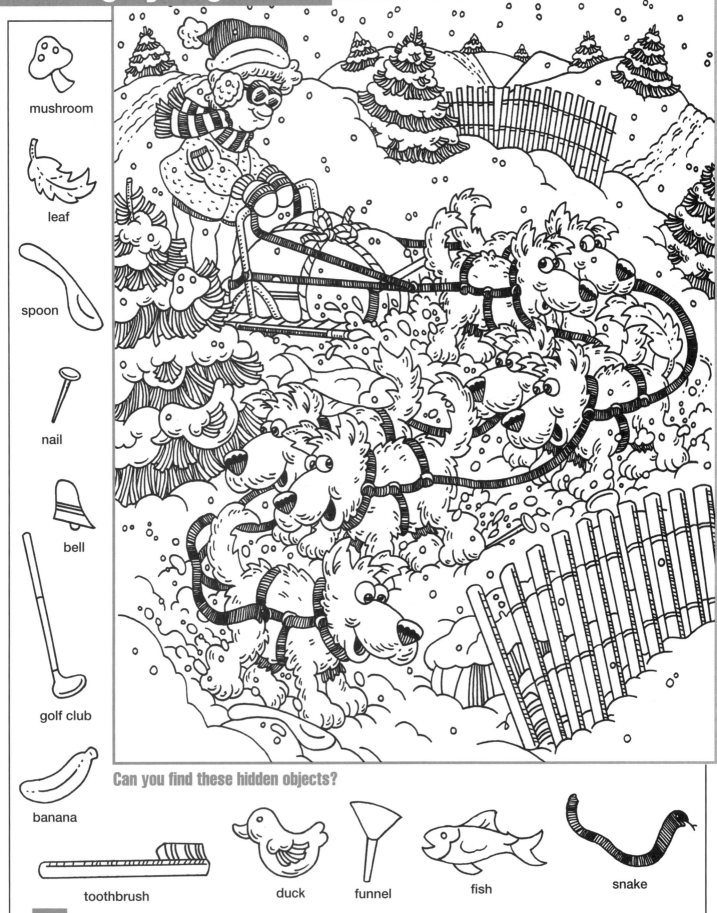

mushroom

leaf

spoon

nail

bell

golf club

banana

Can you find these hidden objects?

toothbrush

duck

funnel

fish

snake

Highlights®

Summer begins on June 21.

needle

musical note

tack

snake

banana

candle

slice of watermelon

nail

teacup

heart

ring

slice of pizza

Can you find these hidden objects?

pear

fork

artist's brush

slice of pie

carrot

pitcher

key

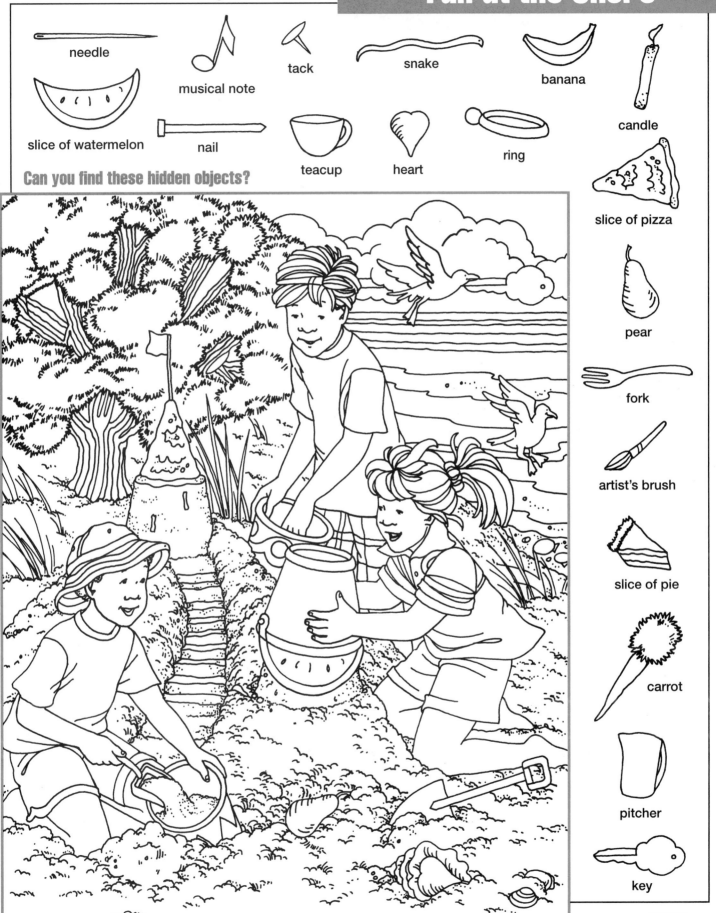

Illustrated by Sally Springer

Highlights®

In 1955—50 years ago—Rosa Parks, a black woman, refused to give up her seat to a

radish

eel

ruler

snail

domino

drinking straw

bowl

saltshaker

carrot

2 bananas

bell

slice of lemon

baseball bat

rolling pin

star

crown

tac

Can you find these hidden objects?

...white man on an Alabama city bus. For many, this marked the
beginning of the civil rights movement in the United States.

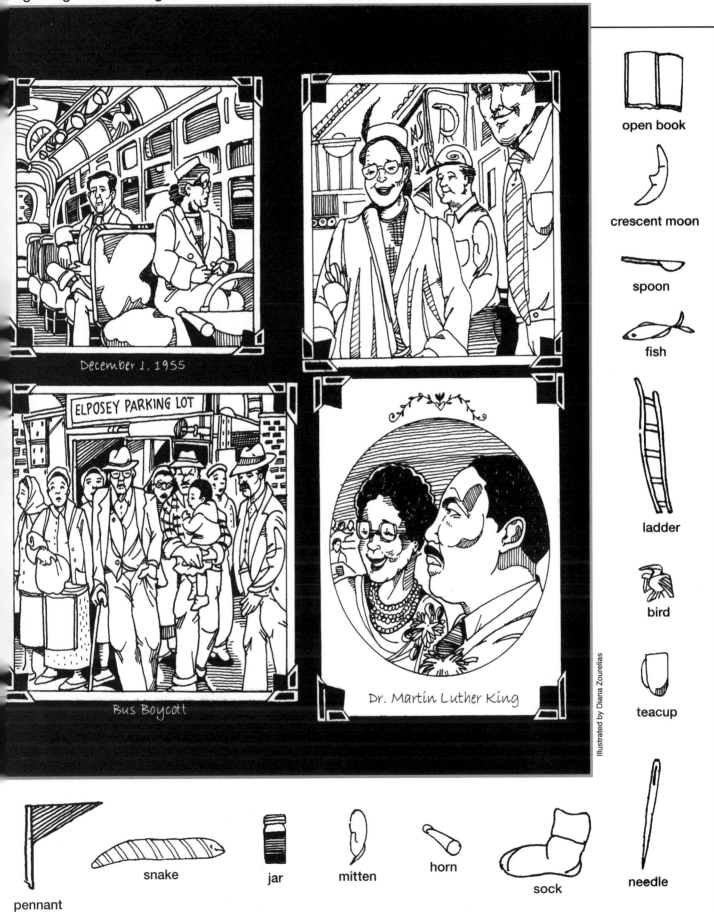

December 1, 1955

ELPOSEY PARKING LOT

Bus Boycott

Dr. Martin Luther King

Illustrated by Diana Zourelias

open book

crescent moon

spoon

fish

ladder

bird

teacup

pennant

snake

jar

mitten

horn

sock

needle

Highlights®

April is National Car Care Month.

slice of bread

football

ice-cream cone

banana

slice of pizza

hot dog

Can you find these hidden objects?

glove

flashlight

pencil

nail

tack

slice of pie

snake

hamburger

Highlights®

This volcano in Washington State erupted 25 years ago in 1980.

Mount St. Helens

envelope

ice-cream bar

carrot

mallet

closed book

Can you find these hidden objects?

flag

eyeglasses

fork

slice of pizza

spoon

trowel

candle

butterfly

artist's brush

Illustrated by George Wildman

Highlights®

11

Charity Bake Sale

spoon

sailboat

button

sock

slice of lemon

worm

mushroom

Can you find these hidden objects?

ring

banana

ruler

mug

leaf

hat

Highlights®

Fireside Artist

ring

tack

eyeglasses

saucepan

coat hanger

artist's brush

spoon

screwdriver

ink bottle

mouse

caterpillar

carrot

Can you find these hidden objects?

shoe

scissors

candle

nail

key

pencil

nib-tipped pen

Illustrated by Linda Weller

Highlights®

November is Peanut Butter Lovers' Month.

ring

eyeglasses

cane

shoe

artist's brush

comb

Peanut Pulverizer

JELLY

Can you find these hidden objects?

flag

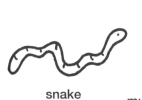
snake

musical note

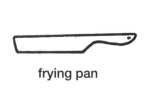
frying pan

mallet

safety pin

crescent moon

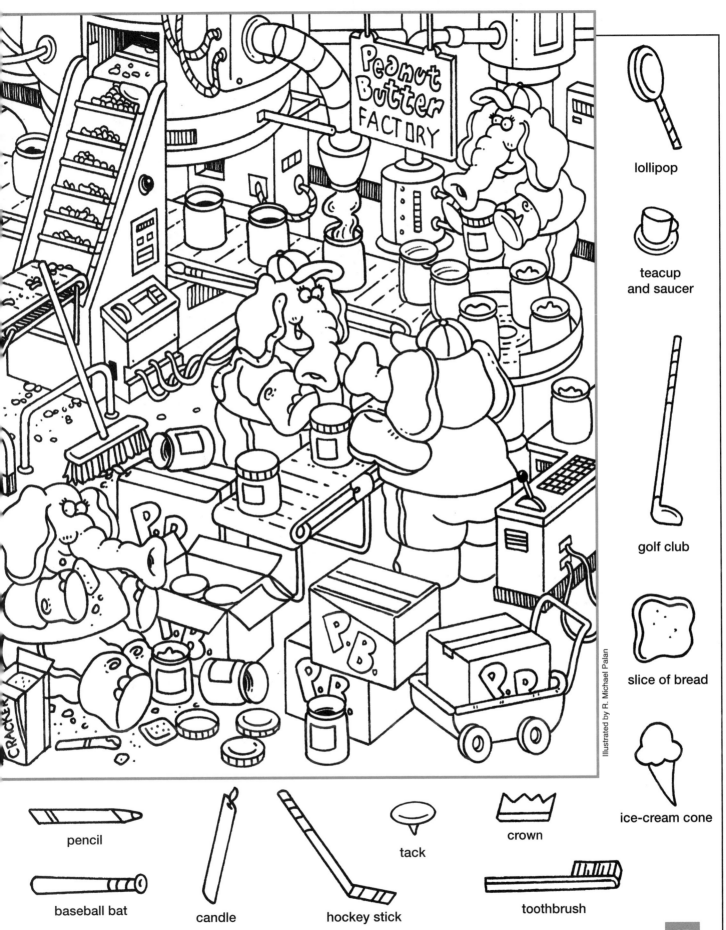

lollipop

teacup
and saucer

golf club

slice of bread

ice-cream cone

pencil

tack

crown

baseball bat

candle

hockey stick

toothbrush

Illustrated by R. Michael Palan

Highlights®

Finding Pluto

The planet Pluto was discovered by astronomer Clyde W. Tombaugh in 1930—75 years ago.

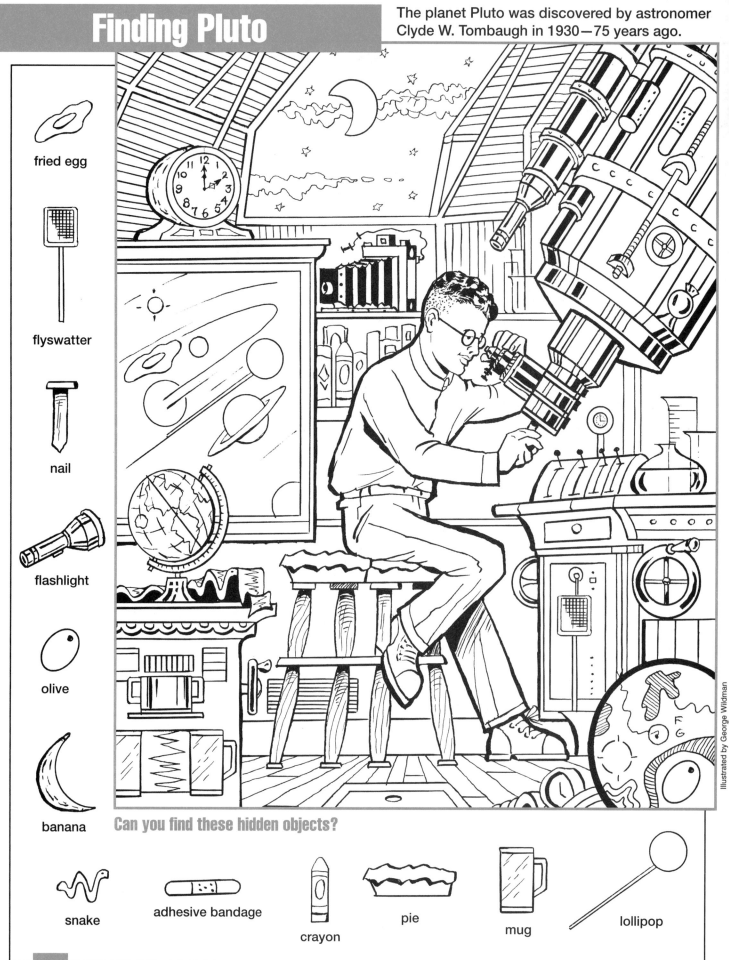

fried egg

flyswatter

nail

flashlight

olive

banana

Can you find these hidden objects?

snake

adhesive bandage

crayon

pie

mug

lollipop

Illustrated by George Wildman

Highlights®

Mother's Day Surprise

spoon

coat hanger

knitted hat

hoe

spatula

artist's brush

tack

tweezers

Can you find these hidden objects?

slice of pie

rabbit's head

needle

candle

teacup

pennant

ax

Illustrated by Lynn Adams

Highlights®

needle

tack

wishbone

toothbrush

ice-cream bar

banana

artist's brush

Can you find these hidden objects?

slice of pie

drinking straw

clothespin

duck

pliers

crayon

mushroom

Illustrated by R. Michael Palan

Highlights®

Buzz Aldrin, the second man to walk on the moon, will turn 75 this year. He was born in 1930.

squirrel

paper clip

in-line skate

bell

sailboat

crown

toothbrush

eyeglasses

Can you find these hidden objects?

ASTRONAUT EDWIN "BUZZ" ALDRIN JR.

nail

ring

crescent moon

comb

banana

Illustrated by Timothy Davis

Highlights®

Christmas is on a Sunday this year.

bird

ice-cream cone

mitten

handbag

tulip

sailboat

Can you find these hidden objects?

crescent moon

pitcher

mushroom

musical note

fork

banana

tack

frying pan

toothbrush

Illustrated by Maggie Swanson

Highlights®

Arbor Day is on Friday, April 29.

toothbrush

mushroom

artist's brush

Can you find these hidden objects?

ice-cream cone

fish

shoe

ice-cream bar

boot

needle

golf club

hat

pennant

ladder

candle

jar

Illustrated by Linda Weller

Highlights®

21

Just Buggy

button

toothbrush

glove

sunglasses

rabbit

sock

football

Can you find these hidden objects?

cat

muffin

scoop

needle

artist's brush

crescent moon

mushroom

banana

Illustrated by Susan T. Hall

Highlights®

Cellophane tape was introduced
75 years ago in 1930.

open book

eyeglasses

mug

golf club

banana

bagel

sailboat

Can you find these hidden objects?

sock

tack

fishhook

toothbrush

envelope

Highlights®

Scooter Delivery

nail

magnifying glass

golf club

candle

Can you find these hidden objects?

ice-cream cone

toothbrush

key

mallet

ice-cream bar

spool of thread

safety pin

celery

Highlights®

March is National Craft Month.

Can you find these hidden objects?

flower

spoon

comb

sailboat

toothbrush

needle

handbell

paper clip

banana

heart

mushroom

shoe

bird

October 2–8 is Squirrel Awareness Week.

ice-cream bar

magic wand

paintbrush

slice of cake

fishhook

Can you find these hidden objects?

sock

mitten

pencil

pushpin

spoon

flashlight

eyeglasses

Ice-Cream Treats

dragonfly

mitten

crown

goblet

lollipop

snail

hat

ruler

banana

pear

butterfly

nail

spool of thread

teacup

bell

Can you find these hidden objects?

Mouse Village

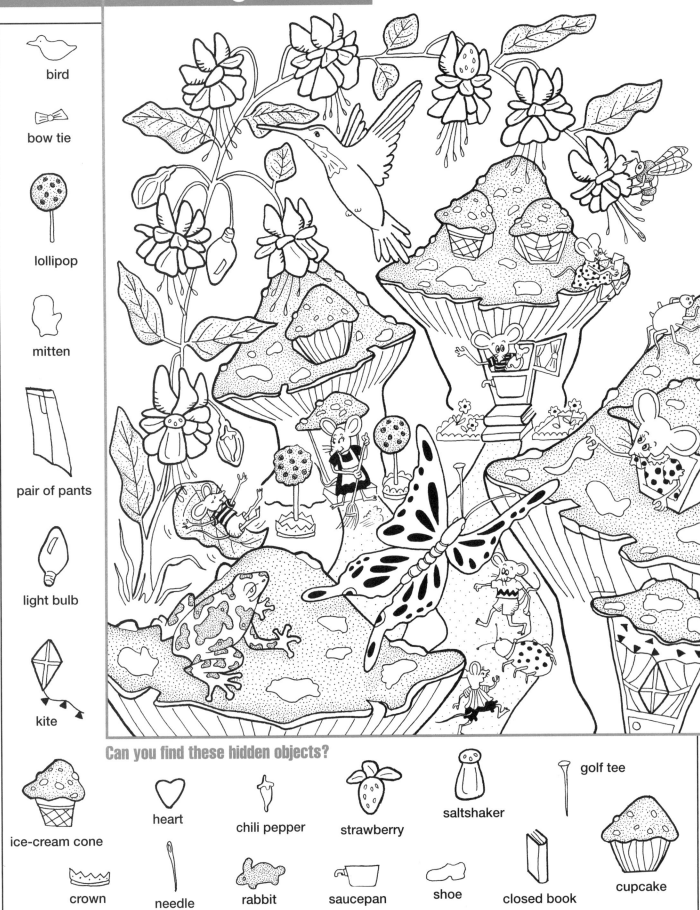

bird

bow tie

lollipop

mitten

pair of pants

light bulb

kite

Can you find these hidden objects?

ice-cream cone

heart

chili pepper

strawberry

saltshaker

golf tee

cupcake

crown

needle

rabbit

saucepan

shoe

closed book

In 1855—150 years ago—U.S. inventor Isaac Singer patented the sewing-machine motor.

Sewing Made Easy

ring

sailboat

snake

paper clip

needle

flowerpot

golf club

paper airplane

egg

Can you find these hidden objects?

flag

2 crowns

slice of pie

ice-cream cone

spatula

Old-Time Car Show

chair

pushpin

magnifying glass

hammer

thimble

rabbit

Can you find these hidden objects?

bird

sheep

cat

slice of lemon

coat hanger

flashlight

gavel

paper clip

Highlights®

eagle's head

heart

crown

wristwatch

teacup

spoon

saw

banana

paper clip

Can you find these hidden objects?

feather

comb

artist's brush

toothbrush

kite

plate

Billy Goat's Garden

2 mice

eyeglasses

fish

hairbrush

pennant

Can you find these hidden objects?

bird

duck

arrow

dragonfly

ice-cream cone

turtle

sailboat

hammer

Highlights®

toothbrush

pitcher

bird

golf club

tube of paint

mushroom

slice of pie

baseball bat

comb

artist's brush

mouse

boot

spoon

sailboat

nail

clothespin

party hat

fishhook

flashlight

Can you find these hidden objects?

Highlights®

comb

crescent moon

teacup

spoon

sock

pennant

Can you find these hidden objects?

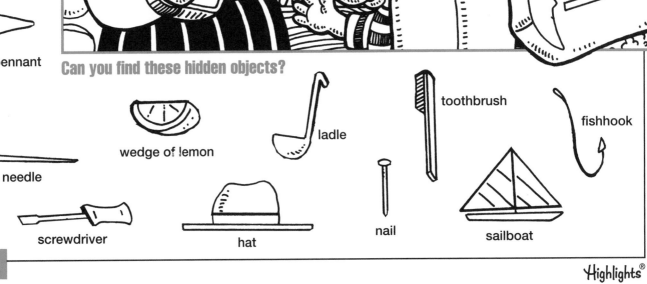

wedge of lemon

ladle

toothbrush

fishhook

needle

nail

sailboat

screwdriver

hat

34

Highlights®

The composer was born on December 16, 1770
—235 years ago.

spool of thread

canoe

heart

nail

drinking straw

tack

flag

pennant

toothbrush

comb

Can you find these hidden objects?

golf club

pencil

candle

snake

needle

beetle

Highlights®

National School Bus Safety Week
is October 16–22.

pear

paintbrush

jar

crown

carrot

candle

R SCHOOL

Can you find these hidden objects?

slice of pizza

wishbone

flashlight

needle

snake

flowerpot

tube of toothpaste

shoe

Highlights®

candle

funnel

ice-cream cone

shoe

teacup

saw

baseball cap

mushroom

fork

Can you find these hidden objects?

banana

sailboat

crescent moon

heart

cupcake

Illustrated by Maggie Swanson

Highlights®

37

Harvest of the Season

broom

doughnut

fishhook

flower

tea bag

Can you find these hidden objects?

fork

pear

sock

ring

crescent moon

flag

ladder

pencil

needle

Highlights®

Answers

▼Page 1

▼Page 2

▼Page 3

Highlights®

Answers

▼Page 4

▼Page 5

▼Page 6

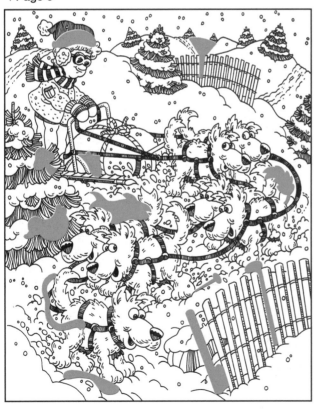

▼Page 7

Highlights®

▼Pages 8–9

December 1, 1955

ELPOSEY PARKING LOT

Bus Boycott

Dr. Martin Luther King

▼Page 10

▼Page 11

Highlights®

Answers

▼Page 12

▼Page 13

▼Pages 14–15

▼ Page 16

▼ Page 17

▼ Page 18

▼ Page 19

Answers

▼Page 20

▼Page 21

▼Page 22

▼Page 23

Highlights®

▼Page 24

▼Page 25

▼Page 26

▼Page 27

Answers

▼Page 28

▼Page 29

▼Page 30

▼Page 31

Highlights®

▼Page 32

▼Page 33

▼Page 34

▼Page 35

Highlights®

Answers

▼Page 36

▼Page 37

▼Page 38

▼Cover

Highlights®